GOD'S GRACE IN HISTORY

GOD'S
GRACE
IN
HISTORY

CHARLES DAVIS

SHEED AND WARD : NEW YORK

Nihil obstat: Joannes M. T. Barton, STD, LSS, Censor deputatus; Imprimatur ✠ *Georgius L. Craven, Episcopus Sebastopolis, Vic. gen.; Westmonasterii, die 18a augusti 1966. The nihil obstat and imprimatur are a declaration that a book or pamphlet is considered to be free from doctrinal or moral error. It is not implied that those who have granted the nihil obstat and imprimatur agree with the contents, opinions or statements expressed.*

CONTENTS

PREFACE

THREE lectures, each of an hour's duration, is a narrow compass in which to examine the complex problem of the Christian attitude to the modern secular world. To have treated the problem in all its ramifications was impossible. The positive though limited contribution attempted in these Maurice Lectures may be seen and judged from the text given in this book. But it will avoid misunderstanding if I point here to some of the questions reluctantly though necessarily omitted.

Making a distinction between secularization (the assertion of the place and value of the secular) and secularism (the exclusion of the sacred or transcendent), I have treated the former but not the latter. Several remarks make my own attitude to secularism plain, but I have not directly confronted its fundamental objections to the Christian faith. This is not because I regard these objections as trivial and unworthy of attention. Far from it. I think they demand detailed consideration. My purpose, however, was different. I have tried to interpret the process of secularization in the light of Christian principles, and in this way to reach a deeper understanding of the working of God's grace in history. My reflections upon the modern secular world are therefore based upon a frankly orthodox Christian faith. I suggest, however, that those who do not share my presuppositions may find the book useful as an hypothesis or test. It offers an affirmative answer to the question whether the Christian believer may consistently welcome the emergence of the secular and the personal and social developments that have created the modern world.

Secular and sacred have here been contrasted from the point of view of human knowledge. This has led in dealing with the secular to a great stress upon the kind of knowledge exemplified by science and technology. I should regret if this were taken as a depreciation of the other forms of human meaning —the world of art, the sphere of subjectivity and personal relations, the various expressions of man's ultimate questionings and yearnings. These are rooted in human nature prior to grace, and thus have a secular aspect. But as I explain in the course of the book, human life when taken in its concrete totality is never exclusively secular. The distinction between secular and sacred, or nature and grace, is important for our understanding of man as he actually exists and the complex order in which he lives, but both come together in the concrete unity of human life. The more fully an activity engages man in his concrete existence and personality, the more difficult it is to discriminate nature from grace. For example, the openness that underlies enduring personal relationships of love is, I should maintain, an openness to the sacred. In establishing the general distinction between secular and sacred, I have therefore been led to stress those more specialized activities in which the secular as such is more clearly manifested. Although I have stated universally applicable principles, a fuller treatment would more closely examine the relation between nature and grace in the deeper and more personal areas of human experience.

The analysis given of the mission of the Church should ideally be accompanied by an examination of what the Church has actually done in the course of its history. The findings would not be entirely favourable. I have mentioned the long and honourable tradition of social Christianity, which illustrates the principle that the Church should act as a dynamic moral and social force. But there is another side to the picture. The Church has not infrequently stood against measures of social justice and reform and identified itself with an unjust *status quo*. The mission of the Church is a task laid upon its members, but they do not always fulfil it. However, although the history of the Church is marred by shortsightedness and stupidity, injustice and selfish complacency, the authentic Christian tradition remains, I should argue, discernible amid the many vicissitudes experienced by God's consecrated people. My concern has been to relate that authentic Christianity to the new situation of the modern world. Despite the frequent historical references, the mission of the Church is therefore seen chiefly as a matter of aim and principle, of what should be. Nevertheless, I recognize that a comprehensive historical investigation, an examination of what has been, is needed for a fully convincing presentation of the Church's role.

The diverse reading that went into the preparation of these lectures makes it difficult for me to trace and acknowledge my debt to various authors. I should, however, gratefully mention the influence upon my thought of the writings of Fr. Bernard Lonergan, S.J., in particular his great work *Insight: A Study of Human Understanding* (Philosophical Library, 1957). Some of the key theoretical concepts and principles I have used are borrowed from him. I have, however, taken them from their original context and applied them to a new question. Hence, I cannot hold him responsible for my conclusions.

Finally, I must express my deep appreciation to the Council of King's College, London, for honouring me with the invitation to give the Maurice Lectures. I am particularly conscious of this honour as the first Roman Catholic to receive it. I should like to think that the generous ecumenical spirit of the invitation is reflected in the lectures it has stimulated. I want also to record my thanks to the Dean, Canon Sydney Evans, whose kindness made the giving of the lectures a pleasure.

CHARLES DAVIS

Heythrop College
Chipping Norton
Oxon.

I

SACRED AND SECULAR

CHRISTIANS today are faced with two interrelated processes. The first is secularization, which may for the moment be described as the massive assertion of the autonomy of the secular. The second is dechristianization, understood in the strong sense as a general loss of Christian faith. The two processes are contemporary with each other; historically they have developed together. It can hardly be denied that they are not just parallel but interrelated. The same causes would seem to be at work. Further, they have the common feature that both are attempts to shake off the tutelage of the sacred. Are they, then, two sides of one and the same process? Is secularization identical with dechristianization? If so, the West is now undergoing a single cultural development. Viewed positively, this is the assertion of secular reality: viewed negatively, it is the rejection of the Christian faith.

When secularization is thus interpreted, it merges with secularism. Secularism as commonly understood is agnostic humanism. Empiricism usually underlies it. Secularists are by conviction anti-metaphysical, and generally exclude any knowledge of what lies outside the range of empirical verification. This is irreconcilable with Christian faith. Christians believe in God as transcending the world and man; they believe, too, in grace as a divine communication transcending nature and reason. Neither agnosticism nor self-sufficient humanism is compatible with Christian faith. The secularist, therefore, rejects Christianity, though he may retain some elements as of value for a humanist. For him, secularization is the advance of secularism. The discovery of the world as secular is the recognition of the universal validity of empirical methods. Modern man is leaving behind the Christian faith as he emerges from his pre-scientific childhood and casts off his metaphysical and religious illusions.

Some Christians would agree with the identification of secularization and dechristianization. Unlike the secularists, they deplore the process. They lament the secular outlook of modern man. For them, the secularization of the West is the rejection of the Christian heritage on which Western civilization was built. They see it as the destruction of Christian values and the spread of a modern paganism. United in their negative attitude to the modern secular world, they speak less clearly and coherently in positively advocating the restoration of a Christian order. Few now simply see the Middle Ages as normative. Logically, however, they have to defend the ideal of a sacral order, that is an order in which the sacred exercises a direct hegemony over the secular.

Other Christians have adopted a different attitude. Increasingly, secularization is being accepted by Christians as a positive and welcome development. With seeming paradox, they see it, not as the enemy, but as the legitimate outcome, indeed the mature fruit, of Christianity. The Church should not oppose the modern secular world, but should recognize its own child in the adult it fears and enter into a different though still necessary relationship with it. The loss of faith which secularization has carried with it is due to the outmoded form in which Christianity has been and still is presented. The Christian faith should be disengaged from the trappings of a past sacral culture and from the thought-forms of pre-scientific thinking. If this is done, the essential Christian message will speak to modern secular man and be acceptable to him. He will not have to renounce his adult status as a secular man in order to embrace the Christian faith.

The recent attempts to reconcile Christianity and the modern secular outlook have raised many problems. The first is to determine the meaning of secularization. The various definitions offered show the difficulty of the problem. Is there a viable distinction between secularization and secularism? I should myself regard some of the Christian writing in this field as a mistaken attempt to reconcile Christianity with secularism, not just with secularization. Again, how is Christianity to be embodied in a secular culture? Is a Christian order no longer an ideal? Further, what is the mission of the Church in a secular world? If the secular city in its autonomy is the result of Christian teaching, what function now remains for the Church? Does secularization mean that the age of religion is past? If so, what place is left for a Church distinct in structure and function from the world?

The literature on these problems is already considerable, and the flow of new books shows no sign of slackening. I shall not attempt to give a survey of all this writing. Nor is it my purpose to enter into a direct discussion of the views propounded by others. The aim is the more modest one of offering some personal reflections on the problems involved in secularization. I hope that what I shall say will contribute to a discussion that will engage the attention of Christians for some years to come.

The first lecture will be concerned with the distinction between the sacred and the secular and will attempt an analysis of secularization. The second will turn to the problem of integrating the sacred and the secular. The third will discuss the mission of the Church in the light of the conclusions reached.

While, regretfully, I must disclaim any great knowledge of the thought of F. D. Maurice, in whose honour I am privileged to give these lectures, I do not think I am wrong to suppose that the theme would have met with his interest and approval.

The antithesis between the sacred and the secular is primitive. It is found in all cultures. Elusive as the antithesis is, an attempt must be made to delineate it. The secular or profane is the sphere of immediate reality. It is what lies open and present before man as truly known by him. He can master it intelligently because it comes totally within human grasp. The sacred is the unknown beyond. It lies higher or deeper than immediate reality. Man cannot master it. He may indeed by magical devices attempt to manipulate it for his own purposes, but this only underlines that it is outside his ordinary control. The sacred is grasped only obscurely. Hence it is usually apprehended and expressed symbolically.

This rough delineation suggests that we define the secular in terms of its intelligibility for man. The secular is that area of reality the intrinsic intelligibility of which lies within man's grasp. It is constituted by all that yields its inner meaning to his scrutiny. Man may as yet know it only in part, but in the field of the secular all is in principle knowable by human intelligence. All is subject to human investigation, and man expects to unlock its intelligibility, so that this becomes evident to his mind. Because the secular is thus what man can understand, it is the area of reality over which he can exercise a practical mastery. His actual powers of control may be very limited, but in principle man's intelligence enables him to dominate what he knows and direct it to the ends he chooses.

The sacred lies outside man's understanding and control. Though it urges itself upon man, its inner nature remains hidden. It does not lay open its intrinsic intelligibility under his scrutiny. Man fails to master its secret and reduce it to an evident object of his knowledge. What is properly sacred is in principle beyond man's understanding; it is not simply a question of what still remains to be understood. But further discussion of the meaning of the sacred must come later. The immediate concern is with the secular.

What, then, is secularization in the light of the definition I have given of the secular? Secularization is obviously the widening of the area of the secular. If the secular is what is intrinsically intelligible for man, secularization is the bringing of an area of man's experience within the range of his understanding. Various areas, previously mysterious, are made subject to man's intelligent mastery, and consequently to his practical control. The process is not identical with the progress of knowledge. An area of experience becomes secular when man recognizes it as in principle within the range of his intelligence. He regards it as having an immanent intelligibility accessible to his investigation, even if his actual knowledge of it is still elementary. What constitutes the modern secular outlook is not the greater knowledge of modern man, but his critical appropriation of his own intellectual powers, expressed in the formation of the principles of scientific method. The social sciences, for example, may be in their infancy, but man is confident that social experience may be understood by empirical investigation. The social has an intelligibility he can reach; it will yield its laws to his scrutiny. To the extent to which that is truly so, human society is a secular reality.

More and more areas of man's experience have become secular in the sense defined. The process would seem to be a pushing back of the sacred, and one is led to ask whether the sacred will not be eventually eliminated. This is the conclusion of some, who, by an extrapolation, deny the sacred altogether. The secularist at least denies that man need take any account of what is not secular, that is, of what does not in principle lie within man's intelligent grasp and control.

But the process can be interpreted otherwise. It may be seen as a process of differentiation. Certainly, much that man formerly regarded as sacred has now become secular. But when man saw almost everything as sacred, he was confusing the sacred and the secular; or, to put it more fairly and accurately, he still had an undeveloped and undifferentiated consciousness. To overcome all confusion of sacred and secular, to differentiate clearly between them, enhances the sacred as well as the secular. Perhaps, indeed, it was a better concept of the sacred that gave the secular its autonomy. What may have happened is not the driving back of the sacred by the secular, but the expulsion of the secular from the sacred.

It has been argued with some reason that it is Christianity itself with its exalted view of the sacred, with its insistence on the true transcendence of the sacred, which has been the fundamental cause of the secularization of the West. The secular was released, because the Christian faith forbade men to identify the sacred with nature or man. I shall come back to this point in a moment. But first let me observe more neutrally that a clear differentiation between the secular and the sacred, with a frank recognition of the autonomy of the secular in its own sphere, does not harm the sacred but rather enhances it. Modern secularization, if properly interpreted, may be regarded as a purification of our concept of the sacred. To sacralize natural forces or society is not only inimical to modern science, but also a denial of the Christian faith. With undiscerning enthusiasm for a unified view of the world, Christians sometimes proclaim that Christianity has abolished the distinction between the secular and the sacred. This is in fact untrue, both historically and theologically. Christianity introduced, and doctrinally requires, a radical distinction between the two realms. It unites the secular and the sacred in a unity of order, but it refuses to identify them.

To turn, then, to the fact of secularization. However various may be the analyses and interpretations
it provokes, the secularization of the West is an
undeniable fact. Great areas of man's experience
have been desacralized and freed from religious control. They are now seen as having an inner consistency and intelligibility of their own, enabling
them to be understood, developed and controlled
without appeal to the sacred, the numinous or the
religious. Although earlier cultures saw periods of
religious decline, the radical secularization of the
West is without parallel. Why has the Christian
West alone given birth to a thorough-going secular
culture? As I have already mentioned, several writers
have argued that the emergence of a truly secular
culture is the result of the impact of the Christian
faith on man's cultural development. Secularization,
they say, is implicit in the biblical revelation of the
Old Testament and is still more strongly present in
the clarification and completion of this by Christ.
What we are experiencing is the working out of the
implications of the Christian fact. Christianity is the
ferment of the revolutionary West. It is a cultural
iconoclast, breaking down the enclosed sacral cultures of mankind. The medieval effort to contain it
within a new sacral order failed. The medieval synthesis was destroyed by its own inner contradictions.

Once Christianity has freed man, he would not again be imprisoned in a closed sacral culture, even when this was named Christian. The open, secular culture of the modern West, with its restless, ongoing movement and recurring crises of growth, with its refusal to make any stage of development absolute, is the effect and authentic reflection in human history of the Christian revelation. That the secular West should now by its impact be breaking up the great sacral cultures remaining in the rest of the world is, despite appearances, an extension of Christianity's influence and a necessary preliminary to Gospel preaching.

That is the thesis of Professor van Leeuwen's book, *Christianity in World History: The Meeting of the Faiths of East and West*.[1] He argues his case by giving an erudite account of world cultural history. On a much more popular level, Professor Harvey Cox has written on the biblical sources of secularization in his book *The Secular City*.[2] To claim secularization as a historical product of Christianity is indeed becoming a commonplace. Earlier writers linked various features of the economic, scientific and technological development of the West with

[1] Trans. by H. H. Hoskins. Edinburgh House Press, London, 1964.

[2] New York, Macmillan, 1965.

Christian influences. More comprehensive theses are now favoured. We are being invited to see the secular West as a legitimate outcome of Christianity, a further stage in Christian history. Naturally, this concerns the broad fact and does not prevent a discrimination among the elements making up the modern world.

I find the historical thesis attractive, but I do not wish to argue it. Undoubtedly it contains much truth. The Christian distinction between Church and State, for example, has undeniably been the decisive factor in the emergence of the secular State. But I suggest that the thesis as a whole requires a much more thorough historical investigation. Historical generalizations are notoriously subject to *a priori* distortion when distinguishing movements and assigning causes. Western culture is a complex of elements. The Greco-Roman as well as the Judaeo-Christian went into its making. The tension between the two traditions will have produced results inexplicable by either alone. Account, too, must be taken of the natural dynamism of human intelligence. Limited as man is by his environment, individual genius can still introduce new factors, which go on to have incalculable effects. Further, it is possible to maintain that secularization would not have taken place in the West without the presence of Christianity, while at the same time denying its

Christian character. A factor in a given situation may provoke a reaction inimical to itself. On the other hand, to judge a cultural development as advantageous to Christian progress is not to prove that Christianity was its cause. It is a well-known characteristic of the Christian faith to profit from each new historical situation imposed upon it and under external stimulus to display fresh potentialities.

I want, therefore, to leave the historical question aside (apart from some remarks on the distinction between Church and State) and dwell more on the intrinsic compatibility of secular culture with the Christian faith. Whatever the causes of the secularization of the West—and I am prepared to allow Christianity a large part in the process—it can, I believe, mark an advance of the Christian faith. It challenges Christians to purify their concept of the sacred and achieve a unity of secular and sacred which does not confuse but clearly differentiates them.

To examine in turn various areas which have become secular:

First, the West has secularized nature in the sense of the material world. Nature is no longer sacred; it has been desacralized. It is now regarded as in principle fully within the range of man's understanding and intelligent control.

Nature was formerly approached with awe and

reverence. The divine or numinous was not clearly distinguished from the cosmic order and its laws. The material world was seen as the embodiment and epiphany of the sacred. Various natural phenomena were interpreted as hierophanies. So closely were the natural and the divine brought together in a single cosmic order that the ordinary processes of nature were charged with the numinous and man's ordinary use of nature became a sacred activity. Agriculture, for example, demanded, indeed in a sense was, a religious ritual.

All that has changed. The scientific and technological progress of the West rests upon what has been called a disenchantment of the world. Nature is a secular reality and requires no appeal to the sacred and religious for its understanding and use.

The scientific tradition rigorously excludes any recourse to transcendent forces in explaining material processes. Man's knowledge of nature is still incomplete, but science has developed a set of methods for seeking the immanent intelligibility of material reality and confidently pursues its investigation of the universe without any thought of allowing for mysterious causes outside its range. It assumes that it can eventually find an empirical explanation for every natural phenomenon. Any appeal to a transcendent principle to fill in a gap in present knowledge is radically unscientific. Newton lapsed from scientific rectitude when he brought in God to complete his explanation of the solar system. Laplace gave the correct scientific reply when he said, "I have no need of that hypothesis."

The technology of the West likewise rests upon a desacralization of nature. Nature, it presupposes, is open to man's exploitation. No longer is it regarded as sacred and untouchable. This is an inevitable consequence of man's scientific understanding of nature. Nature ceases to be mysterious. What man intelligently masters, he proceeds to dominate and control. Recourse to religious ritual becomes irrelevant.

Now, this secular view of nature, which is fundamental to science and technology, is in full harmony with the Christian faith. I would go so far as to say that it is required by it. Any other view of nature is, in the light of Christian teaching, idolatrous, superstitious or magical.

The Christian God is Creator. That means that he is distinct by transcendence from everything else. Transcendence is not an image of God, but an affirmation about him. What, then, is affirmed? First, that God is not to be identified with the universe or with anything that is part of it. Second, that he is the total origin of everything. All other beings have a derivative reality; they are his creatures. He alone is absolute and not dependent. A transcendent cause is a total cause. God, therefore, cannot be brought within the cosmic system. His causality is not a factor, however important, existing alongside other factors in the network of relations and laws studied by science. To say that God is Creator is to postulate a relation of total dependence of everything upon God, but this does not affect the internal structure and laws within the universe itself. God cannot be assigned a place within the universe; his causality cannot be reduced to a particular function within a general scheme. Precisely because his causality is total, it does not appear when what is sought is the intelligibility inherent in the universe itself. God is indeed immanent in the universe, but as its transcendent cause not as part of its system. He is not anywhere in particular. He has no determinate place. He is everywhere as the ultimate ground of everything. The scientist studying the correlations within the universe does right to prescind from God. This simply respects God's transcendence. Science takes the fact of the universe for granted, and studies the evolution and structure of the reality before it. The question of God does not arise when the scientist is temporarily at a loss to furnish an explanation of some feature within the universe, but when men ask why there is a universe at all. Such a question is outside the scope of science, which must presuppose its own object.

Because of a current confusion of terms, it is well to note that the doctrine of creation has nothing to do with the scientific question whether the present order of the universe results from a process with a beginning or is maintained by an endless process. Creation is a relation of total dependence upon God. What it affirms is as true of the universe in its present state as it is of its past history. There is no necessary link with the question whether the universe as we know it had a beginning or not. Scientific theories about the origin of the universe do not in fact raise the question of creation in its philosophical and doctrinal sense. And scientific proof or disproof of creation in that sense is a logical impossibility.

The transcendence of God, therefore, leaves nature as a secular reality, a reality which can be studied for its own sake without reference to his presence and action. This leaves untouched the question whether God in acting in human history for man's salvation manifests his action by miracles. These by definition are exceptional and their meaning is discerned only by reference to the moral order of salvation. They leave intact the intelligibility of nature as studied by science. Any such events are for the scientist occasional enigmas he can safely ignore.

The Christian faith supports the scientific enterprise also by maintaining that God is a wise and intelligent cause. Underlying science is the conviction that the universe is intelligible. As long as it was seen as at the mercy of arbitrary deities needing appeasement, science was impossible. Christianity asserts the unlimited intelligence of a God who acts by design not by caprice. What he creates is therefore entirely intelligible. Since God is total cause, unlimited by factors outside himself and of infinite intelligence, he does not need to correct his work nor intervene to remedy some unnoticed defect. We may conclude that the material universe as created by God has within itself all the potentialities required for its full development as planned. Science may seek to unravel that development and its laws. No interference by God will upset its findings. The subordination of the material world to man's destiny and its consequent integration into a higher order raise further questions requiring separate handling. The point here is that material phenomena have their immediate explanation within the universe itself, and there are no divine interferences perfecting the material universe within its own order and affording an explanation of the otherwise inexplicable. To suppose that there are is to hold an unworthy idea of God.

Technology, too, harmonizes well with Christian belief. For the Christian, man is made in the image and likeness of God and has dominion over the lower creation. His intelligence comes from God and is a share in the light of the divine intelligence. Through it he takes an active part in God's plan for the universe, and is intended to dominate and control his environment. He moulds the universe to serve human destiny, because God made it for man and put man over it. Man rightly endeavours to subject all material creation to himself, since it is through him that it is to be directed to its end.

The problem of technology does not lie in any untouchable sacredness of nature, but in the moral responsibility of man. Men must not exercise their dominion in an arbitrary or selfish manner, but as an intelligent and responsible stewardship. In brief, they should do so in a way that recognizes the needs of all men and all the needs, not just material satisfaction, of men.

Thus, the secular view of nature, which lies at the basis of modern science and technology, is quite compatible with the Christian faith. Indeed, it would seem to be demanded by that faith. At the very least, it is far more in keeping with Christian truth than any view that sees nature as the embodiment of the divine, as permeated with the numinous, as inaccessible to man's understanding and outside his intelligent control. Nature itself is not sacred for the Christian.

Most Christians would now accept the general contention that nature is a secular reality. But there are persistent relics of an earlier sacral view. Perhaps the most notable is the conviction that all life is sacred. How often do Christians assert that science will never unlock the secret of life, because this is God's special domain! The processes of life, they say, are sacrosanct, inaccessible to scientific understanding and not to be manipulated by technology. A view increasingly difficult to maintain! Human life undoubtedly has an inviolability, which is the consequence of the inviolability of the human person. But what is at stake is the dignity and rights of the human person, not a sacred mystery surrounding life. The origin and processes of life are within the range of man's investigation and eventual understanding. Over this domain also he will exercise an intelligent control, which should respect the hierarchy of values and the rights of the person. There is no call to make a special appeal to God to explain life, nor are its physical processes peculiarly sacred.

The second great area of man's experience which has become secular is the political and social order. Clarity demands separate consideration of the secular State and secular society.

I have already remarked that the secular State is manifestly a product of Christian history. To glance at that history is the best way of determining its meaning and assessing its relation to Christian teaching.

A great innovation of Christianity was to introduce a distinction between Church and State, which meant a distinction between the religious and political spheres, between sacred and secular authority. The distinction was based on the conviction that the mission of the Church came from God through Christ and was not subject to the authority of the State. This contention radically limited the power of the State, which before had always extended over the whole of human life.

The distinction is an essential element in Christian teaching, but it has had a chequered history. At first it was clear in an unreflective way. Christians resisted the claims of the pagan Roman State. The conversion of Constantine caused confusion. The Emperor assumed a paramount role in the Church as well as the State. The popes, however, resisted the claims of the eastern emperors over the Church, and the failure of imperial rule in the West gave the Western Church its freedom. But the development was checked by the establishment of the Holy Roman Empire and the claims of the Carolingian and German emperors. Western Christendom was formed as a politico-ecclesiastical unity. The duality of authority within its structure inevitably led to conflict. With the reforming popes of the eleventh century there began the long struggle between Pope and Emperor for supremacy. The popes were fighting for the freedom and independence of the Church, but they in their turn went too far and did not sufficiently recognize the autonomy of the secular. The theoretical distinction between the sacred and secular spheres of authority was in fact worked out in the Middle Ages, but it was not put consistently into practice. There was thus an inner contradiction in medieval Christendom: a theoretical recognition of the duality of sacred and secular, but a confusion between the two spheres in practice by the maintenance of a politico-ecclesiastical unity and sacral culture. This inner contradiction led to the disintegration of the medieval order, the collapse of Christendom and the eventual emergence of the secular State.

The *dénouement* was long delayed. The Reformation brought no fundamental change in the structure of Christendom, but only a territorial and confessional cleavage within it. In each of the confessional regions the politico-ecclesiastical unity of Christendom was maintained as the norm. On the Roman Catholic side, the Church, chiefly owing to the possession of the papal States, was involved in political alliances and manœuvrings. The papacy sought to protect its own territory and also to secure the rights of the Church in various countries by political means. This often meant securing a privileged position for Roman Catholics and denying religious freedom to others. On the other hand, the popes had to suffer the constant interference of Christian rulers in Church affairs.

The breakdown of Christendom came with the Enlightenment, at the end of the wars of the confessional States. The State religions were restricted, but at the cost of weakening the dogmatic tradition of Christianity. The French Revolution launched a secularist State, hostile to the Church. The old political order of Europe was in fact over, though there followed a long struggle to restore it. The papal States were eventually taken over by emergent Italy.

Unfortunately, the papacy did not succeed in freeing itself from political involvement in support of the old order. It cherished the illusory hope of restoring Christendom and opposed the new, liberal forces. This was not altogether surprising in view of the hostility of the liberals to the Church and their rejection of Christian belief and practice. But the mistake was to rely upon political means to preserve the Christian faith and to regard the past order of Christendom as an absolute norm. What was needed was a spiritual revival, which would have purified the Church and enabled it to meet the new situation, distinguishing between the good and the bad in the new ideas. Instead, the political policy of the papacy had the effect of checking the stirrings of such a revival among Roman Catholics, and the Church withdrew into a sterile opposition to the modern world. Eventually, however, the spiritual forces within the Church broke through, and a renewal of the Church began which has steadily gathered momentum. With a new vision of its faith and mission, the Church was able to recognize that the new, democratic freedoms, despite many ambiguities, were a genuine advance in man's political consciousness. What is more important, it came to see the inappropriateness of political pressure as a means of securing the preservation and progress of Christian faith. The Church has now gained a new, reflective awareness of the essential distinction between secular and sacred authority, and has ceased to expect the State, even in a Christian country, to promote the mission of the Church by political means. The function in religious matters of the State is to establish and guarantee conditions of religious freedom for all its citizens, whatever their beliefs, within the limits of public order. While it will recognize the religious life of its citizens as an element in the common good, it has no authority to enter into the sphere of the sacred.

The culmination of this development is the Declaration on Religious Freedom of the Second Vatican Council.

The implication of the new stance of the Roman Catholic Church is that the State is a secular reality. Many would still, I think, jib at the statement. Time is needed for a new idea to work itself out in the mind with full consistency. Fear is aroused by the unfortunate associations of the word "secular." But the logic of the matter will, I am sure, prove inescapable. The concept of the secular State means that the power of the State does not extend into the higher, sacred order of human life. The State is not the judge or representative of ultimate truth concerning the world and man. Its concern is not with the transcendent nor with man's eternal destiny. Its function is limited to temporal and terrestrial affairs, and its powers should not be used for the furtherance of any sacred mission, whether that of the Christian Church or of any ideology that claims to possess ultimate truth about man and the world. A secular State is not secularist, and does not seek to promote secularism. Least of all is a Communist State secular. It is rather a return to the monolithic unity of archaic society, where the State is totalitarian, because the secular and the sacred have not been clearly distinguished.

The State, then, for Christians is not sacred. Political authority comes from God only in the sense in which the entire world, including man as a social being, comes from God. But no State has an immediate divine mandate. All political systems are relative and changing. They come within the sphere of man's developing understanding, and are subject to his intelligent modification and control. Man will order and adapt his political institutions as he orders and adapts the material world. In seeking political change, he is not tampering with the sacred.

Secular society presents a more difficult problem than the secular State. To argue that it is a product of Christianity is paradoxical, and its value seems questionable in the light of Christian teaching. Even were a society entirely Christian, the State would remain secular as exercising a purely secular function. But surely Christians must work to achieve a Christian society and not regard modern secular society as ideal?

I have presupposed the distinction between society and State. When constitutional traditions have developed, the State becomes an agency with a limited role within society. The public authorities, which are invested with the power of the State, are charged with certain limited functions for the benefit of society. These are the functions requiring the coercive discipline of law and political power. They are defined by constitutional law in accord with the consent of the people. Society embraces a wider area, an area of personal and corporate freedom. There is thus a distinction between the common good and public order. The common good includes all the social goods, spiritual, moral and material, which men pursue together. Society as a whole pursues the common good; it is the concern of all its members and corporate institutions. Public order concerns the State, and is precisely the good order to be achieved by public law and political authority. This is not just negative, but includes a positive promotion of the common good by ensuring peace, justice, public morality and material welfare. But it does not embrace all the activities of society, but only those that require the ordering and sanction of public law. The State has an increasing role in the complex and highly organized societies of today, but to deny the distinction between State and society is to make political government totalitarian.

What, then, is a secular society? A secular society is a society or people that has not committed itself

as a society to any particular view of ultimate truth.
The members of the society disagree about the ultimate meaning of the universe and the place of man
in it. It is a pluralist society, including within itself
a variety of attitudes about ultimate beliefs and
values. Unlike a Christian society, it is not based
upon adherence to Christian truth and values. But
likewise the social order is not grounded upon some
other religious faith or on an ideology hostile to
religion. In so far as the common good means the
sum total of the social goods cherished and promoted
by the members of the society, individually and cor-
porately, it includes explicitly Christian beliefs and
values, but also other beliefs and values. But in so
far as the common good is understood narrowly as
the cultural values that must be accepted by the
generality of members if the society is to survive
and social collaboration be possible, it prescinds
from the sacred and religious. The social consensus
is secular not as excluding the sacred but as pre-
scinding from it in building a social order on a
minimum of common principles and aims acceptable
to men who differ profoundly on any question concerning the transcendent or sacred.

The first question that arises is: is a secular society,
truly open and pluralist, viable? It would seem to be
a society without a common culture. The informing

element of culture as an organized way of life is a common, social tradition. A culture is a spiritual community that owes its unity to common beliefs and common judgements of value, transmitted in a social tradition. Without a common culture, does not society disintegrate? A secularist culture would be consistent, but would mark the end of Western values, which are derived from the Christian tradition and dependent upon it. The West is living, it is argued, upon Christian capital. But the present compromise cannot long continue. Either the West will return to the Christian tradition, the chief formative influence of its culture and the foundation of distinctively Western values, or else Western culture will perish. Religion has always been the soul of culture. Some new religion or ideological pseudo-religion will take the place left empty by Christianity. Communism seems the most likely candidate. Society needs some agreed ultimate basis for its values; in other words, it needs the sacred, if only in the form of the secular made absolute.

A second question follows. Can Christians positively accept a secular society as they have accepted a secular State? Surely, they can regard it only as a *pis aller*. While respecting freedom of conscience, they must work, it would seem, for a Christian society, which means a society built upon Christian

truth and values and unified by a common acceptance of the Christian faith. A secular, pluralist
society cannot be an ideal; it does not do justice
to the role of Christianity in the world. From this
viewpoint, the secularization of Western society
must be deplored and efforts made to restore the
Christian West.

Neither of these questions can be tackled until
more has been said about the meaning of the sacred
and the integrating of the sacred and secular as
God's plan unfolds in human history. This is the
theme of my next lecture. Before concluding, however, I want to link secular society to the definition
I have given of the secular as that which displays its
intelligibility to man and lies within his intelligent
grasp and control. I do so by pointing to the problem
of urbanization. This suggests that the immediate
Christian reaction to a secular society over-simplifies
the issue.

Urbanization and secularization go together in
the development of modern society. For that reason,
Professor Harvey Cox finds it natural to treat them
together in his book *The Secular City*. They are in
fact parts of the same process: the bringing of man's
social life under his intelligent mastery. What is
urbanization? It is man's creation of community.
The city is community as the product of man's intel-

ligence. There are human communities that are based on spontaneous tendency; they are cemented by an elemental feeling of belonging together. Such are the family and its expansion into the clan and the tribe. Such, too, are the groups that arise naturally among people thrown together in a common situation. No doubt man has a part in making these communities, but they are essentially given with his nature. They are not the work of his organizing intelligence. Civil community is. It is a complex product, involving a technological mastery of material environment, economic arrangements and political institutions. The man-made structures become increasingly complicated as society develops. Modern urbanization is the rapid spread of artificial communities created by man. They are found throughout the world and are the framework of life for ever greater numbers of men. Underlying them remain the spontaneous communities, but the organized urban community is becoming the dominant and determining factor in social living.

The city is secular as the product of human intelligence. Man's control of his social life is not limited to mastery over the material environment. The many problems that arise in urban civilization are being tackled by the empirical social sciences and the techniques they create. Men are gaining an ever greater knowledge of social laws and social psychology, and are confident they can with eventual success handle all social problems with the methods and techniques of the social sciences. Religion need not enter into the process. Any recourse to the sacred seems incidental, if not irrelevant. And it is a fact that both social scientists and trained social workers find themselves able to collaborate easily on the basis of their specialized knowledge, even when they differ in the matter of religion. Society has become a secular reality because it can be studied and controlled by man's intelligence. Man creates it and controls it. No longer is it sacred and inaccessible. The social sciences are as autonomous in their field as the sciences of nature are in theirs. Any recourse to the sacred to fill in the gaps in present knowledge and technique is regarded as illegitimate.

I do not think that that is the whole story or that the empirical methods of the human and social sciences can adequately explain man. Nevertheless, there is much truth in the contention that human life is subject to empirical investigation and direction. It is simply a question of recognizing the autonomy of the various sciences of man within the limits of their proper objects. No Thomist would have difficulty in admitting this. Human society and man's psychological life may be studied under particular formalities without any reference to the sacred.

This brings me to my immediate conclusion. The present problem of distinguishing and relating the secular and the sacred is, I suggest, a continuation of that process of differentiation within the consciousness of the believer which began with the intellectual effort of the Middle Ages. The Scholastic achievement has often been dismissed as theological dogmatism. It was in fact the vindication of the rights of human reason and the foundation of Western science. Faith was distinguished from reason, and reason left with its proper function intact. There is a contrast here with what happened in Islam, which also tried the experiment of assimilating Greek learning. The experiment failed because the internal conflict between the scientific and religious traditions proved incapable of solution. But in the Christian West, the distinction between faith and reason gave philosophy its autonomy over against theology. Then from philosophy in due course the various sciences asserted their independence. Intellectual attainment became secular because no longer a mere propaedeutic to sacred learning, nor the prerogative of a priestly caste. Parallel to the distinction between faith and reason developed the distinction between grace and nature, through which the believer grasped both the transcendence of God's self-giving love and the intelligible consistency of the creature God made to receive that love. The question of sacred and secular is the problem of transposing the medieval distinctions into a new cultural context. This context has been created by scientific and technological achievement and by a growth of historical awareness with the sense of relativity this brings.

Man understands reality by grasping and formulating distinctions and correlations. His consciousness thus gradually becomes differentiated, and a balanced outlook correspondingly more difficult to achieve. Secularism is a narrowing of human consciousness, a refusal to accept the tensions inherent in a complex and developed mentality. The problem of balance in complexity is solved by suppressing the sacred. The Christian cannot reply by suppressing the secular. He has the more difficult task of respecting the two sides of the distinction, both in theory and in his own life.

2

SACRED AND HOLY

THERE are various ways of handling the distinction between sacred and secular. The method I have chosen is to take as a criterion intelligibility for man. What is secular lies within the range of human understanding. Man may have to struggle hard before he grasps it. To know with understanding is rarely an easy achievement. But the secular is the domain open to human investigation, the field where the enquirer can expect the insight that masters its object and penetrates its intrinsic truth. The sacred remains hidden before man's scrutiny. He is unable to subject it to his understanding. Its intelligibility is not within his grasp. The more he is aware of its presence, the less claim he makes to understand it. Men may deny the sacred; when they admit it, they acknowledge its transcendence.

The sacred, then, is the area of mystery. Not mystery in the corrupted sense of an awkward puzzle, nor in the diminished sense of what yet awaits successful investigation. But mystery in the sense of a presence in man's experience of a darkness he knows to be light but cannot see, of an intelligibility too bright for his gaze, of a transcendence that evokes his adoration. Mystery is the presence of God. Man cannot with truth locate that presence. God is not beyond or outside the world; he is not above or below; he is neither within nor without. His is an undefined presence, which imposes itself upon man's experience without uncovering the secret of divine Being.

To determine man's capability of knowing God is difficult, because in this concrete order no one is left to his own resources to reach God. God, I would maintain, gives his enlightening grace to everyone, and works in each man from the beginning of his responsible life to bring him to faith and love. This is true of the unevangelized, not just of Christians. It has always been true. The faith and love achieved in the unevangelized may be implicit and obscure; its conceptual formulation may be hopelessly confused; the persons concerned may be unable reflexively to analyse their own attitude. But their awareness of God, however they name him, is not a natural knowledge; it is the experience of faith. To delimit, therefore, man's inherent capability of knowing God, we must turn to the theoretical assessments of the philosophers and theologians. A descriptive account of how man actually knows God will not provide a precise answer.

For St. Thomas Aquinas, human reason of itself can tell us very little about God. His thought is summed up by saying that human reason can establish that there is a God, but cannot know what God is. By pursuing his questioning about the universe to the point of asking for an ultimate explanation, man is led to formulate a notion of God. The notion is elaborated by laying down the minimum requirements for the complete intelligibility of all reality. The process is similar to the way a scientist will determine beforehand the conditions the solution he is seeking must fulfil, Reflecting upon this notion and its relevance to the data, man can infer that there is such a Being. He thus knows that there is a God. He does not, however, know God as he is in himself. He has no direct knowledge of God. He has no access to God's intrinsic intelligibility. What God is remains hidden from him. Man knows only that God will in an eminent way fulfil the preliminary notion he has been compelled by reason to form of him.

God, therefore, is not a secular reality. Although, to the limited extent outlined, God comes within the range of human knowledge, he escapes man's under-standing. Man cannot grasp him as he is in himself. He cannot master God's proper intelligibility and make the intrinsic truth of God's Being evident to the human mind. God is at the heart of the sacred. He is the mystery *par excellence*. Everything we rightly call sacred is a communication of God as he is in himself. The secular is the reflection of God in creatures distinct from himself and subject as such to human understanding.

Yet, God did not intend to remain himself inac-cessible to man. He has communicated himself. That is the chief burden of the Christian message. God invites men to a new relationship with himself. Men are already his creatures, dependent upon him and bound to acknowledge him. But the acknowledge-ment possible within the limits of man's own re-sources could scarcely be called a personal relation-ship, because man's natural knowledge of God is so dim. God made men for a more intimate union with himself. He offers men the kind of relationship with him that demands the same life, the sharing of the same happiness, and an interchange of love as within a family or between friends. In brief, he invites men to a personal union, a union that re-alizes, though surpasses, the qualities associated with deep personal love when found among men. The

Christian fact is God's self-giving as it comes to men. Christian revelation is the self-disclosure made by God when he called men into personal communion with himself.

The call of God, though it reaches all men personally, was not addressed to men as individuals but to mankind as a unity. Thus it was given visibly in human history. For men to respond, God must act upon the depths of each man's personality by his Spirit. But he expressed his invitation within the historical process and embodied it in human events and words. The result is sacred history, which is a line of events and their prophetic interpretation, word and event together constituting God's revelatory act.

At the centre of sacred history is Christ. In Christ God manifested his definitive commitment. He spoke the decisive word and gave the final covenant. Despite sin, men would be brought into union with himself. Individuals might still use their freedom to withdraw, but the destiny of mankind and of the universe through mankind was assured. In Christ was also reached the summit of God's self-communication. The man Jesus is the eternal Son of God. He is indeed fully man, the man closest to God, in whom the union of love God willed for all men is fully achieved. But to stop there fails to state his full mystery. He is in person the only-begotten Son, who is one in Godhead with the Father. Through Christ was thus revealed, though yet obscurely, the inner life of God as a Trinity and, consequently, the pattern established of God's self-communication. Men were to become brothers of Christ, sharing by adoption his sonship from the Father, and possessing the Spirit as the gift Father and Son bestow. In that way they were to enter into a personal communion with the Three Persons of the Godhead.

The incarnation placed Christ at the head of mankind. It is by accepting him and joining themselves to him that other men achieve their union with God. But this demands a new community amongst men. God's offer is made to mankind as a whole, and Christ's function is to gather men into a new unity. Personal union with God, therefore, sets up a new network of personal relations among men themselves. They are brought into a unity which is a genuine community of persons, not a mass. The goal towards which mankind is striving in Christ is a unity binding all men together in an interpersonal communion of love. This communion is grounded upon a personal relation between men and God, established by God's self-giving.

I have recalled profound truths with what must inevitably be a distorting brevity. It is not my purpose here to dwell upon them. My concern is to indicate that the mystery of God has been expressed and communicated to men in history. The mysterious sacred has been revealed in the form of sacred history. Further, in Christ and in the Church, his Body, mystery became sacrament, using that word in the wider sense to mean the visible presence of grace, or God's self-gift, in effectual sign and symbol. And the presence of the mystery brings a new force into men's lives, working to transform their existence both individually and socially, urging and enabling men to achieve a new pattern of human living and a new form of human community.

But the sacred keeps its mystery. Despite the revelation made and the communication given, it remains beyond man's understanding. Man cannot grasp it in its immanent intelligibility. He cannot unlock its secret and make it evident. Only in the beatific vision will we directly know God and understand him as he is in himself; only then will we be able to grasp the intrinsic truth of his self-giving. Meanwhile God addresses his revelation to faith. Events are adapted as signs, and the prophets and Christ borrow human concepts, images and words to express their message. These can only convey by analogies a remote idea of the reality of which they speak, and cannot display its intrinsic truth. Hence faith can never be imposed upon the mind by rational argument.

The revelation, however, is enough for God's immediate purpose. He wants a free commitment, not a compelled assent. He acts upon man's conscience and leads him to a conviction that he ought to believe. When a person obeys the summons and accepts the message, he is freely committing himself to God. His faith is not the admission of an evident conclusion from tested premises, but a free response to the offer of personal relationship. Faith is the response that grounds a personal communion with God.

In the light of his experience of faith, the believer will meditate upon God's word. His loving union with God will refine his discernment. He may order his knowledge of revelation, reflect upon it, draw out implications and attempt when useful a reformulation of various statements. Such activity is fruitful; it allows what he believes to penetrate into his mind and enter into relation with the rest of his experience. But he is aware that he has only glimpses of knowledge, that he is, as it were, looking at a confused reflection in a mirror. The sacred is not yet known face to face. His acceptance of it can only be by an act of faith. For that reason the interpretation of revealed truth presents an insoluble problem to unaided human intelligence. It can take place only within a tradition supported by the Spirit, where individual efforts at some understanding and re-formulation are tested by the community. All who seek to interpret revelation by reason alone inevitably reduce it to secular truth and eliminate mystery, namely the sacred.

There is, therefore, an area of man's experience which remains sacred and never becomes secular. There is an element in human life and human history which escapes his understanding. And it is precisely that element which determines his destiny. The mystery of God is present to men. It demands faith and will not be mastered by human intelligence.

Some may wonder that I have not yet used the word "supernatural." It is certainly applicable in this context. The difficulty arises from the misleading associations of the word. With a theological audience, there is no danger of its being taken in the popular sense referring to ghosts and all that. But even theologians are troubled by the spatial imagery it evokes. One would almost suppose some think that the primitive spatial meaning of words made it impossible to adapt them to the expression of non-spatial relationships. Yet, presumably, to say that the king is above the people does not mean that he is spatially elevated above the populace. It is posible to conceive, though not imagine pictorially, a non-spatial relation. The word "supernatural" as used in theology has no spatial connotation.

I should define the supernatural as what exceeds the proportion of nature. A proportion is a set of comparable relations. When taken with reference to man, the proportion of nature is the set of comparable relations which intelligibly link together all the elements, properties and conditions we distinguish when we reflect upon man. The proportion of man's nature is in fact its intelligibility, its consistency as an intelligible unity. The supernatural exceeds that proportion. It does not constitute man's nature, nor result from it, nor is it demanded by it. It is a supererogatory gift from God, which cannot be accounted for by examining what is implied in being a man. Certainly, the natural and the supernatural are not in opposition, and nature should be seen as a receptivity open to God's gift. In the concrete, God made man for the supernatural. But nature is not grace. Grace, which is the supernatural, is proportionate to God's nature not to man's; it is a communication by God of what is properly his own. Grace is in fact absolutely supernatural, which means that it exceeds the proportion, not only of man's nature, but that of any created nature or

natures. The theorem of the supernatural is a formulation of the mystery of God's self-giving. Nature
is indeed open to grace, but to identify them is to
deny that God out of a free, personal love can offer
man the unexpected and unexacted gift of himself.

The Catholic tradition on grace has always insisted that God's self-giving carries a created gift
with it. Grace in the primary sense is God himself. It
is the gratuitous benevolence of God towards men,
his saving love, his justifying forgiveness. What God
gives us, as I have insisted, is himself for our happiness with him in a personal communion. But God's
love is an effectual love, which transforms the person he loves. His communication of himself would
not be made, would in fact be meaningless, unless
its reception was marked by a real change in the
condition of the recipient. Personal union with God
would not be real if it left us entirely as we were
before. God's self-giving, therefore, results in a created grace, which is a transformation effected in
man himself. This created grace is itself supernatural
as exceeding the proportion of his nature. It can be
understood only in relation to union with God as
he is in himself; it is a sacred not secular reality. The
grace of sanctification, with the faith, hope and charity it brings and the repercussions of these upon
man's moral life, constitute a sacred element within

man himself. They mark the presence of the sacred mystery of God as he communicates himself to man. They bring human life and history within the sphere of the sacred.

The differentiation between secular and sacred is an easier task than their integration. But to this I must now turn.

To introduce the subject I want to venture outside my field as a theologian to comment upon the general order discernible in the universe. It would seem that in the universe there is a hierarchical order of successively higher integrations or systems. Each higher integration systematizes what is unsystematic in relation to the preceding system.

The sub-atomic particles fall within a system governed by the laws of physics. But the regular behaviour of atoms is not accounted for by this system, and in relation to physical laws such regular behaviour remains coincidental. The behaviour of atoms is in fact systematized by the laws of chemistry, though in such a way that the more fundamental physical laws are not violated. From the viewpoint of the laws of chemistry, the metabolism and division of cells are mere patterns of coincidences; but they are systematized by the laws of biology. Under biological laws, the distinctive behaviour of animals is a set of coincidences. Animal behaviour is grasped as a system by the laws of sense psychology. Studied as animal behaviour, the intelligent and free activities of man are merely coincidental. They are to be understood by invoking the laws of rational psychology.

Thus, the chemical elements are governed by chemical laws, but without violating physical laws. Plants are governed by biological laws, but without the cessation of physical and chemical laws. Animals are governed by the laws of sense psychology, but physical, chemical and biological laws remain valid. The higher system keeps the lower laws intact, but integrates them into a higher system, to which they become subordinate. Man as an intelligent and moral being is a still higher integration. The laws of physics, chemistry, biology and sense psychology apply to him, but in human living they are subordinate to a higher system.

The transition to man, however, brings two notable differences in the way a higher integration is achieved. First, man is not born with the higher integration of human living already his possession. The synthesis which constitutes a genuine, human, personal life, both intelligent and moral, begins in each man as a potentiality not as present fact. Man has to create an authentic human existence for himself by his own intelligent and free activity. We have to make our lives. Second, the range of man's creative intelligence means that he is not confined for his living to a single, fixed system. So much so, that rather than constituting a higher system, man as intelligent and free is the source of innumerable higher systems. He organizes his life, both personal and social, in a variety of ways. He creates different economic, social and political orders. He develops varying cultures. He can change his material environment. He can alter social customs. He can choose various forms of personal existence. The systems he creates cannot be evaluated by reference to a single, ideal form of human living. There is no such single form. Human living, both personal and social, is an expression of man's free, creative intelligence. He has a choice between good and good, and not just between good and evil.

The need for a distinctively human life to emerge from potentiality and the diversity with which that potentiality may be developed give some explanation of the unique and complex pattern to be found in the life of every individual. But individuals do not develop in isolation. Man is essentially social. He becomes himself only in relation to others. The establishment of the integration we call human living is largely a social achievement. The quality and type of the social environment into which he is born determine the range of choice open to the individual and profoundly affect his personal development. The emergence of the higher system of human life is, therefore, an historical process. The vicissitudes of man's social development are the stuff of history. Man has his being in an historical unfolding. If there is a history of each person, it is part of the larger history of mankind and can be understood only by being placed in that context. To reflect upon the problem of achieving an authentic, human existence is to come up against the problem of the meaning and course of human history.

Mankind's development faces two apparently insoluble problems. These are reflected in the life of every individual, but they can best be considered at the level of history.

The first problem is inherent in the need for development. Man's intelligence begins as a potentiality, and only with difficulty does he struggle towards understanding and knowledge. Again, man does not begin fully equipped with a freedom for action. His will is untrained, and does not exercise a ready mastery over impulses both from within and from without. A process of liberation is required before he is genuinely free. He has to form habits which give him willingness and readiness to act in particular ways. The helplessness of undeveloped man is partly overcome in the individual by education. But education cannot solve the problem when the lack of understanding and defect of freedom are found in mankind as a whole or throughout a particular society. Yet, events do not always wait upon man's development. He is hurried blindly into mistaken decisions or fails to achieve effectual action in time, and disaster follows. "The human crisis," wrote Mr. Raymond Williams, "is always a crisis of understanding; what we genuinely understand we can do."[1] The trouble is that understanding is not always available just for the asking and sometimes can be reached only when it is too late. The collapse of societies in the past illustrates this. If one looks with detachment at the human enterprise, it seems doomed to ultimate failure. The pace of intelligent and moral development is too slow to meet every likely contingency. Sooner or later, a mistake or failure will bring a disaster from which recovery will be impossible. To meet the problem inherent in his own development, man seems to need more than human resources.

And there is a further problem. Men do not suffer only from an imperfect development, but from a wilful irrationality. To express the same point theo-

[1] *Culture and Society*, Penguin ed., p. 324.

logically, they sin. Sin is the irrational in human consciousness. It is the failure of free will to act reasonably. The sinner as an intelligent and responsible person recognizes what he ought to do or what he ought to avoid. He refuses to act in accord with his moral judgement. He introduces an inconsistency between his knowing and his doing. To suppose that every human problem can be met by understanding is to overlook that for sinful man knowing the good does not always mean doing it. The Christian revelation has told us more about sin than otherwise we should know. We are now more aware of its ravages and of its impact upon the course of history. We know something of its origin. All this is very relevant to a Christian view of history. But it is not necessary to be a Christian to acknowledge the fact of sin, to admit that men can and do wilfully refuse to conform their actions to what they know to be right. Everyone can confirm the fact by examining his own conscience.

Add the inevitability of death, and the two problems I have outlined take form as the tragedy of human life. Human life is tragic. Early promise is constantly blighted, and there are the irretrievable blunders of ignorance and impotence. Worse still, his own wilful folly besets man, and few have not had to endure the thought that they have destroyed when they knew they should love. Death would seem to be the appropriate signature to human life as it is. Does it not underline the ultimate failure and meaninglessness of human endeavour?

A criticism made of much fashionable Christian writing is that it is falsely optimistic. I do not wish to risk unfairness by saying that the criticism is justified. But it is certainly true that any superficial optimism does not correspond with human experience. The working out in the concrete of the problems I have sketched in bloodless abstraction has been the theme of a great part of human literature. No account of human existence and the possibilities for human progress rings true if it hides the darker side of life and the reasons for human despair. And it is particularly unfitting for a Christian to encourage such pretence, because he preaches the message of the Cross.

The Cross indicates the manner in which God has solved the human problem. He has not done so by sweeping it aside. That is why we still experience it, though we live in a redeemed world. Instead, he has initiated a scheme of reversal, a process of transformation. The scheme of reversal primarily concerns sin and its consequences. Sufferings and death are in this present order the consequences of sin. They become through the Cross the means of overcoming sin and obtaining salvation. This, then, is the reversal. There is sin, having its origin in man's freedom. Sufferings and death are its result. These, willingly borne in union with Christ, are the road to salvation. Death, with all it symbolizes, is transformed into life. The transformation was first effected in the death and resurrection of Christ, and then through the power that flows from the risen Christ the same transformation takes place in other men. The scheme of reversal, which is the law of the Cross, is the governing pattern of human history.

But the same redemptive force that overcomes sin is the solution God offers for the problem of general human inadequacy. The light of faith and the strength of grace are the means available to man to ensure that human development does not in fact end in meaningless disaster. The assurance that mankind will come through its crises and will eventually, despite human ignorance and weakness, reach its destiny is an assurance based on faith. History will reproduce the pattern of the Cross, but the Resurrection is the promise of success. The secular owes its preservation to the sacred, and through it achieves its intended development.

God, then, has through Christ introduced a solution to the problems of human living. But the solution he has given is a transcendent gift. This is a

point, it seems to me, often overlooked by Christian
writers on the secular. Instead of solving man's problems on the merely human or natural level, God in
answering human problems has given man a still
higher integration for his life. What, positively
speaking, is the gift of salvation? It is the self-communication of God and the resulting supernatural
pattern of human living I have already described.
Man is now destined to live not just as man could
live from his own resources but as a child of God,
in a personal communion with God, sharing his life,
called to know and love God as God knows and loves
himself. The union with God profoundly affects
man's personal way of living, giving him a new discernment and a higher set of values. At the same
time, it works to bring about an interpersonal communion among all men which is of a degree and
quality higher than their common humanity would
demand or could achieve.

In other words, Christianity comes as a new and
higher system or integration of the life of men, and
an integration which cannot be achieved by human
resources alone but must be achieved as a gift from
God. As a higher synthesis of human living, the
order of grace integrates and subordinates all the
lower systems found in man, without however destroying them. They remain intact, as the system of

chemical laws remains intact when brought under a biological system. All the innumerable systems, ordering human life and created by man's intelligent and free activity, keep their proper functions and their distinctive laws. The technological, economic, cultural, social and political systems, with the intelligible relations they imply, with their distinctive laws, proper values and purposes, are not denatured by grace. In so far as they are the product of man's intelligence, they are subject to man's intelligent understanding and control. They can be studied by the various, autonomous, empirical sciences without appeal to the sacred. Each system has an inner consistency of its own and laws proper to itself. Scientific understanding of the nature and laws of a particular system gives rise to techniques for its practical handling. These techniques are justified within their particular spheres without higher reference. All these systems for human living, with their variety and complexity, constitute the secular dimension of man's existence.

To distinguish this secular dimension from the sacred is necessary if both are to be respected. Those who reduce man to an animal and attempt to explain his rational and free activity exclusively in terms of sense experience distort human experience. Likewise guilty of distortion are those who treat man as an angel and forget that his rational and free activity is based upon sense experience and conditioned by it. Distinguish in order to relate is the only way to be true to reality in all its complexity. Thus, the autonomy of the secular in its own sphere should be recognized, but without eliminating the sacred. There is no difficulty in doing justice to the secular, provided it does not claim to be the whole of human life. The Christian contention is that the final and total integration for man, to which all the lower systems are subordinate, is the order established by God's grace.

The lower systems keep a relative autonomy. But what is true is that the higher the system, the greater its repercussions upon the lower systems it integrates. Chemical laws do not make much difference to the behaviour of the sub-atomic particles. But consider the effect of sense life upon the biological system in animals. An animal organism still obeys all the laws of biology, but the complexity and refinement of its biological system is explicable only by its subservience to sense psychology. The higher system has adapted and perfected the lower system, though without violating its laws. In keeping with this general law by which a higher system not only introduces a new integration but also perfects the lower systems on their own level, we should expect

Christianity to have a profound effect on all areas
of human life. By being drawn into a new total pattern, each sphere of human experience is perfected
and refined in itself. The order of grace has considerable repercussions upon the secular areas of
man's life, perfecting them not destroying them.

In emphasizing this influence of grace, there is a
constant temptation for Christians to swamp the
secular in the sacred and not allow the secular its
proper place and function. To ward off this temptation, a further distinction is useful. I borrow it from
Fr. Chenu.[1] The distinction suggested is between
the sacred and the holy.

The word "sacred" is linked with the word "consecration." Now, consecration in the strict sense is
the withdrawal of a thing from its ordinary use and
purpose, in order to dedicate it to God, to his worship or service; or, when applied to a person, the
withdrawal from his ordinary social commitment
and situation to an exclusive dedication to God, so
as to be wholly at the disposal of his worship or
service. To be sacred or consecrated would thus imply withdrawal from the secular. It would mean the
cessation of the ordinary use or purpose of the thing,
of the ordinary commitment of the person. To urge

[1] M. D. Chenu, O.P., "Consecratio mundi," *Nouvelle Revue
Théologique,* 86 (1964), pp. 608–18.

in this sense the consecration of the world would be to advocate a sacralization—the cessation of the secular in favour of the sacred.

The word "holy" does not have the same implication. What is made holy may keep intact an ordinary use and purpose if a thing, an ordinary social commitment and situation if a person. Sanctification is not the same as sacralization. When the secular is made holy in this sense, it keeps its consistency and function on the secular level. To sanctify the secular is to bring it within a higher order, while retaining its consistency, value and function. It is not made a mere means to a higher end, but keeps its relative autonomy as an intermediate end.

The phrase "the consecration of the world," frequent in recent writing on the lay apostolate, is ambiguous. It could, but does not in fact, mean the sacralization of the world, with the cessation of the secular as secular. The meaning intended is the sanctification of the world, with the secular remaining as secular but brought under a higher order. Notice that the higher order is the order of grace, not the ecclesiastical order of the institutional Church. The Church as an institution does not exercise a hegemony over the secular.

So, when we consider the Christian order in its total range, we should distinguish the sacred and the sanctified. What is sacred is not secular. Either in itself it transcends the secular or it has been removed from the secular sphere by consecration in the strict sense. God in the self-giving that founds the Christian order and then the created gifts of grace that result from that self-giving are sacred of themselves. Sacred by consecration are the persons and things that in varying degrees are withdrawn from the secular to become more or less exclusively the visible signs and instruments of the sacred. The area of the consecrated, limited in extent, makes possible an express symbol of the sacred, an epiphany, as it were, of its presence in the world. The institutional Church constitutes this area, though for most of its members only a small part of their lives is set apart from the secular for the exclusive service of the sacred. The sanctified as distinct from the consecrated is everything else, the whole reality of the world and of human life, in so far as it has been brought under the higher order of grace. The task of the Christian is to sanctify the world, not strictly speaking to consecrate it. The use of the word "consecration" reflects an early Christian habit, found in the Bible itself, of applying the vocabulary of cult to describe the more general process of sanctification.

The analysis I have so far given of the relation

between sacred and secular is not enough. Taken by itself it would make their relationship too static. The dynamic element of history has now to be brought into consideration.

The Christian order is not imposed or offered all at once in its completion. As a higher integration of human living, its growth and achievement form an historical process. Its emergence is an historical development. The sacred is given in a sacred history. But further, the historical unfolding of salvation does not replace the ordinary process of human development; it transforms and completes this. Just as any higher integration, the order of grace presupposes the lower integrations and is conditioned by them. This is only another way of restating the old adage that grace persupposes nature. The modern awareness of man's historicity compels the interpretation that grace presupposes nature, not just in the static sense, but in the dynamic sense of historical development.

Since Christianity was introduced as tendentially a world order, which from its beginnings would work to bring about a higher integration of human living, culture and thought, it could have been given only when the human race was sufficiently advanced for it. God could not have given the Christian message, established the Christian Church and inspired the Scriptures during the earlier stages of man's history. Unless we suppose a miracle that would in fact have replaced the actual order willed by God with some other, the gift of Christianity had to wait upon an appropriate stage of social development. And because the Christian order is an integration not a destruction of human life and growth, its spread and efficacy are conditioned by the limitations inherent in man's historical development. The possibilities of missionary endeavour have always been determined by the contemporary human situation and contemporary cultural and material means. The historicity of man determines the manner in which the sacred is made present in human life. Man would not be man if he did not achieve his destiny in a social and historical unfolding. God's gift of a supernatural destiny has respected the human condition. The Christian revelation, which offers that destiny, was given in human history after an historical preparation. Men's knowledge and acceptance of it, their understanding of its message, their application of this in their lives, and the working out of all its implications for every area of human existence are achieved only in an historical development. And this sacred history presupposes and is conditioned by the secular historical process, according to which man develops the potentialities inherent in his nature. Certainly, the final Kingdom will surpass all that goes before, even the Christian preparation for it. It will be a judgement upon history and a gift of resurrection. But just as the incarnation in an unexpected way surpassed its preparation and yet demanded and fulfilled that preparation, so, too, the final Kingdom, while surpassing its preparation, still demands it and will fulfil it.

The new awareness of the historicity of Christianity has caused a confusion of terminology. Because the word "secular" comes from *saeculum*, the Latin equivalent of the Greek word *aion*, which means age, period or era, secularization is interpreted as the discovery of the dimension of time and history. It is then possible to say that Christianity is secular, with the meaning that it is historical in the full sense of realized within the ongoing process of human history. There is no point in quarrelling about words. I have found it clearer to start with the distinction of sacred and secular and to interpret the secular as nature and the sacred as grace. There is sacred as well as secular history, intimately related though these are.

To return to the question of historical development. History is an open-ended process. By this I mean that at any given time or in any given situation there are always a number of alternative possibilities for the next stage. Will there be progress or decline, consolidation or collapse, fruitful advance or fruitless stagnation? Any particular state of affairs might evolve in various possible directions. No fixed, systematic laws determine which selection of possibilities is actually fulfilled. Events do not follow an invariable, determined sequence. To hold that they do would be a determinist view of history. Such a view finds little support in historical fact. And God's providence does not imply that he could have created only a determinist order. The kind of order he created is to be discerned by reflecting upon the actual historical process. There we find that the connection between possibilities and realizations is nonsystematic. The course of history is not predetermined by systematic laws that allow no divergence.

Nevertheless, there is an order in history. Were our knowledge more extensive, we should be able more frequently to calculate probabilities, grounding the schedule of expectations upon the factors present in the particular situation. However, although a sound estimate of probabilities may give us a true insight into the state of affairs, it is not falsified by the occurrence of the less likely. Actual fulfilment may diverge from the order of expectations, and the least probable may sometimes happen.

But what remains true is that concrete possibilities of development only gradually emerge and do not exist at an earlier stage. There was no concrete possibility of space flight before modern science had reached a certain stage of development. Successful democratic institutions presuppose a certain degree of social consciousness. At a given stage of history, particular developments are not concrete possibilities. They have no probability at all. They will become probable only after various prior stages have been completed. To expect them at an earlier stage is in effect to deny the reality of historical development; it is to take a radically unhistorical view of man.

Christianity, as I have said, is inserted into the historical process. Christian achievements and Christian aims should, therefore, be judged in the light of the historical moment to which they belong. This, I suggest, provides the only sound approach to the problem of the Christian attitude to modern secular society. It is tempting to argue that, because all men should be Christians and Christian influence should permeate society, secular society must be deplored. The argument is invalid because it omits to consider the historical situation. In doing so, it refuses to accept the law for Christian development established by God. On its premises, only the final Kingdom, not the preparation for it, would be positively acceptable. However, when the Christian society of the Middle Ages and modern secular society are both viewed from the standpoint of Christian history, secular society does not appear as the evil some Christians suppose.

The Christian society of the Middle Ages was a partial, premature achievement, the breakdown of which was highly probable. It was partial, because it did not rest upon the free, personal adherence of the multitude to Christianity, but was established and maintained by political and social compulsions. It was premature, because the personal and social consciousness of ordinary people was not sufficiently developed for the achievement of a Christian society in the full sense. It was unstable, because it was torn by inner contradictions, particularly the confusion between the sacred and the secular. There was such a stress on the sacred that secular reality was not given its proper place in human life, either individual or social. The tension this provoked came to a head in the conflict of political and ecclesiastical authority.

In saying all this, I am not condemning the Middle Ages. To do so would show a lack of historical sense. Judged in the light of the historical circumstances, the Christian achievement of the Middle

Ages was striking in many respects. But medieval society under the surface was far less Christian than romantic historians painted it. Recent, more sober assessments show better both the strength and the weakness of the medieval synthesis. More credit is being given to the medieval contribution to humanism by its idea of human dignity, its defence of reason and its desacralization of nature. The modern world has more roots in the Middle Ages than it cares to admit. At the same time, the superficiality and corruption of popular religion and the failure of Christianity to do more than gloss over many pagan social customs and attitudes have become more evident. Medieval Christendom was an imperfect, first attempt at a Christian order; it was doomed to failure from the outset.

This casts light upon the dechristianization of the modern world. How far is it a loss of genuinely Christian faith? The faith lost by the average man in the West was an imperfect faith, what might be called a cultural faith. The Christian tradition, superficially understood, was simply accepted as part of the culture in which one lived, taken for granted with the social environment. This situation did not do justice to the transcendent quality of Christian faith, which cannot be reduced to an element of human culture, nor was it true to the mean-

ing of faith as a free, genuinely personal response
to God. Indeed, the so-called dechristianization of
some areas is simply an awakened Christian awareness of the absence of faith there. Historical studies
by religious sociologists in France have shown that
some of the dechristianized rural areas have not
been properly Christian for centuries, if they ever
were. And is it not truer to say that the great industrial cities were never Christian rather than that
they have lost the faith? So, while no doubt the
present absorption in the secular has drawn many
from the faith and increased the power of secularism, the general dechristianization of the West
is not the destruction of faith by secular culture. It
is the uncovering of the defects in Christian evangelization, the breaking down of the political and
social façade that hid those defects, and the consequent purification of the Church for a renewal of its
spiritual mission.

In the world situation of today, where Christians
are a proportionately decreasing minority, what social context offers the best chance of carrying out
the Christian mission? The answer, I suggest, is a
pluralist, open or secular society. When men differ
as they do about ultimate truth, the only acceptable social order is one in which men do not try to
impose their beliefs upon others by compulsion,

whether physical or political or social, but decide to live in harmony on the basis of intelligent reasonableness, a willingness to listen to others and discuss problems, a desire to reach agreement by persuasion and a constant respect for all individuals and groups. Within such a society, a free, personal faith can develop, and Christianity make its proper appeal, untrammelled by a social influence that does not correspond to the spiritual development of individuals. The social effects Christianity achieves will rest upon a genuine social consensus and ultimately upon a personal assent of faith. A pluralist, open society is far from secure in the modern world. The question of its viability has still to be answered. But it does represent a genuine ideal in the present historical situation. It implies a new respect for human dignity and personal freedom, which provides an excellent context for Christian faith. As secular, it allows the full emergence and appreciation of secular human values, which can easily be stifled by a one-sided stress of Christians on higher values. Granted the limitations of human insight and judgement, the slow acceptance of Christian beliefs and values seems necessary for the eventual achievement of a balanced synthesis between secular and sacred.

In brief, to deplore secular society and work for

its immediate replacement by a Christian society is to misjudge the present moment of history. It would imperil the very conditions for the development of Christianity, both by encouraging other groups to seek with equal precipitation to impose their ultimate convictions upon others and by neglecting to assimilate the new understanding of the secular in its distinction from the sacred.

What, then, should be the mission of the Church at the present time?

3

THE MISSION OF
THE CHURCH

WHEN the question of the Church's role in modern secular society is raised, the immediate and understandable reaction is to observe how ill-adapted to its present tasks are the existing structures of the Church. It is not surprising, then, that a flood of books should have appeared on the reform of Church institutions. I am myself convinced that this is an area which calls for radical thinking.

Admittedly, the Catholic tradition has always maintained that the constitution of the visible Church is not just a matter of human devising. As well as leaving his followers a body of teaching and a set of rites or sacraments, Christ, it is asserted, established a pattern of social authority for the Christian community. But so often this has wrongly been taken to mean that the Church has a single, unchanging institutional structure. The rise of historical studies has here had a liberating effect. These studies have shown how relative ecclesiastical institutions are., The same pattern has been embodied in greatly differing structures in different historical epochs.

Examined from a sociological standpoint, the early Church was a federation of local Churches. This federal structure passed in the West into a feudal setup. Then from the high Middle Ages to Trent gradually emerged the centralized, absolute monarchy with which Roman Catholics are familiar. Within the Roman Catholic Church, the period from Trent to Second Vatican has been dominated by an absolutist system, according to which almost all authority is derived downwards from the top. This system is now breaking up. A new structure is being gradually formed, which will eventually replace it. As far as one can discern its features, the emerging structure will give much greater place to the principle of representation, to local independence and responsibility and to a separation and wider distribution of functions.

The extent of the changes now under way is worrying many. They fear a weakening of the God-given institutions of the Church, particularly of the papacy. It needs perhaps stressing that no area of the Church's life has been more affected by secular ideas and practices than the use of authority. In itself authority within the Church is *sui generis;* strictly speaking, it is not monarchical nor oligarchical nor democratic, but has similarities to all these secular orders. The embodiment of Church authority in concrete institutions has always reflected the predominant social environment, with the result that now one, now another feature of its complex pattern has been thrown into relief. This process should not be confined to the past. I see no reason why the Church should have to exercise its mission in the modern world with an institutional structure proper to an age that is past.

What is true is that no one can draw up a blueprint for the future. Development and change must take place within the continuity of Christian tradition. Each past stage has enabled Christians to grasp better some aspect of the Church's reality. Further development, while leaving aside the incidental features proper to a past situation, is never a repudiation of previous advances in Christian understanding. The Church is not a man-made organization, but a community given by Christ and sustained by his Spirit. It is a question of discerning the indications of the Spirit and then acting upon these with a boldness that overcomes human timidity and inertia. Christians need both the humility of faith

to refrain from treating the Church as a secular
reality they can organize at will and the courage
to shake off familiar but antiquated customs at the
summons of the Spirit. The Church is always ad-
vancing into an unknown future, but from a base
consolidated in the past.

Reflection upon the problems facing the local
Church in an urban society reveals the same need
for change. Present parochial organization is pa-
tently inadequate. It is insufficiently adapted to the
social patterns of urban and industrial environment,
and consequently fails to relate Christian faith and
activity to the actual life of modern men. Even for
Christians, the Church becomes marginal to their
ordinary working and social lives, and Christian
witness is impaired because out of touch with the
real problems of modern society. A reshaping of
local Christian organization is called for. Parishes
must be at least supplemented by other groupings.
Secular social structures and relationships are increasingly complex; the problems they raise require
advanced social techniques. The Church has to me-
diate grace to men in society and bring the sacred
to bear upon the present social realities of secular
life. Unless the sacred is related to the secular, it
cannot exercise its integrating role. To establish a
fruitful relationship in modern conditions, the

Church must evolve more flexible and more complex institutions and groupings. The simple all-purpose territorial unit is not enough. The use of religious sociology with its scientific study and techniques is essential.

As soon as such problems are broached, the question of the ministry arises. What should be the shape of the ordained ministry? Should the full-time ministry be complemented by various part-time ministries? Since the Constantinian settlement, clergy and people have been distinguished as two social classes. Is this kind of social embodiment now desirable or even feasible? Part of the present problem of the ministry is that the clergy are losing their social identity. Their function within the Church is ceasing in secular society to carry any social status with it; it does not give them a recognizable place in society at large. Psychologically they are troubled, even if often unconsciously, by a sense of isolation from society. But if priesthood alone does not provide social identity in a secular society, how far is secular commitment or even political involvement compatible with priestly office? An additional secular pursuit distinct from priestly function is at least a better solution than a secularization of the sacred ministry by reducing it to a form of social work.

Within the Church itself, the new understanding

of lay function and responsibility is affecting the understanding of the priesthood. A change in the place and role of the laity is inevitably a change in the place and role of the clergy. To solve these problems it is not enough to point to the distinctive sacramental role of priests, clearly marked out as this is in the Catholic tradition. Taken in the concrete, priesthood always demands a particular though changing embodiment both within the Christian community itself and in relation to society as a whole. The cessation of Christendom and the emergence of secular society will have the unavoidable result of altering the outward form or social shape of priesthood. People overlook, I think, how much the present shape of the priesthood is not the pure expression of its sacred function but the embodiment of this in a social role proper to a past social order—and to that extent a secular rather than a sacred phenomenon. The experiment of worker-priests has had the good effect of raising most of the relevant questions, though answers are not so readily available.

To discuss the detailed problems of change in Church structures and organization lies outside the scope of this lecture. Impatient though one might be with the slowness of the Church to adapt itself to modern conditions, the abundant literature on the subject shows a widespread awareness of the problems. Little good would be done by my attempting here to formulate summary solutions. My chief concern is with the fundamental problem that underlies all the particular questions, namely, what is the mission of the Church in secular society? In other words, what is the role of the Church? What should the Church be trying to do?

But before I turn to this problem, a further observation about Church organization is called for by what I have already said about secular society. Life for a Christian in a secular society means a great stress upon free, personal faith. He is no longer carried along by social environment. That is the advantage of a secular society. It provides an occasion for purifying and strengthening Christian faith. It allows faith to assume its proper character as a free, personal commitment. But it would be equally a distortion of faith, if the individual believer were left in isolation. Hence the imperative necessity of forming primary groups among Christians. A primary group in the sociological sense is a group where the members personally know one another and are involved in an intimate, face-to-face association and co-operation. When Church and society coincided, there was little need for concern with

Christian primary groups. The primary groups that arose from ordinary social intercourse provided sufficient Christian interchange and support. That is no longer true. And not all can be left to the family. This is often insufficiently Christian, and, in any case, the more limited function of the family in modern society renders it inadequate as the sole primary group for the Christian. The urban parish with its large numbers is necessarily a secondary group. A secondary group, sociologically speaking, is a wider association, not resting upon immediate personal encounter, but held together by common beliefs and values, by the expression of these in language and symbol, and by a unity of administration. The weakness of the Church at the moment is that its structure of secondary groups has no adequate basis or support in a corresponding structure of primary groups. Consequently, since primary groups are fundamental in forming the social personality and ideals of the individual and since secular groups do not give the distinctive Christian contribution, the Christian faith has only a weak hold upon the lives of many people who sincerely call themselves Christian. Without primary groups, Christianity cannot strike deep roots. Living in a secular society, Christians should form such groups for the maturing of their faith. Of their nature these groups will be small, interpersonal and requiring stimulus rather than organization.

At the same time, unlike some writers, I should regard the Eucharist as belonging more properly to the secondary than to the primary group level. I should not want to lay down a hard and fast rule here; all the sacraments permit great variation in their mode of celebration. But the Church is a wider community, not a sect. The chief function of the Eucharist is to unite and express the full community of the Church. It does not just seal the intimacy of those already united by personal association. The effect of the Eucharist is to join those who celebrate it to the mystical community of the one Body of Christ; they enter into communion with Christians everywhere, indeed with the saints already in glory. Granted that the Eucharist can be celebrated only as a local assembly at a particular time and place, it is all the same a general gathering of Christians united in faith and public worship, not a meeting of intimates. It expresses and mediates a wider community than a primary group. Primary groups are the outcome of the Eucharist rather than the appropriate context for its celebration. They are the result of practical efforts to give particular

and concrete embodiment at the immediate interpersonal level to the universal Christian fellowship
achieved by the Eucharist.

Some of the writing on Christian community in-
dulges a romantic nostalgia for the simplicity of
rural civilization. The complexity of the populous,
urban, industrial society of today will necessarily be
reflected in the community structure of the Church.
It is illusory to suppose that Christians can achieve
an actual I-Thou relationship with all their fellow
Christians. Relations in general among Christians
will be more distant and more functional. To make
general demands for intimate togetherness is to impose an impossible burden and equivalently to reject the structure of modern urban living. There is
a danger of making Christianity appeal only to social
inadequates and of offering the Church as a refuge
from the strains of urban civilization. Certainly
those who for any reason are crushed by the city
must receive our love and attention, and Christians
should strive to eliminate the inhuman features of
urban life. Part of the contribution of Christians
will be to promote spiritual and personalizing values
and to resist the reduction of all social life to economic activity, a reduction that can make a modern
city unfit for human beings and an instrument for
their destruction. But urban society as such is a

complex achievement of human intelligence, intended to enhance the possibilities for human living. Those who can meet its requirements should find a Church related to their real lives, not one that in effect demands a return to the structures of rural living.

But it is time to raise the question why there is a Church at all.

There has been a pretty far-reaching change in the understanding of the Church's mission. It springs from the recognition that the order of grace is not confined to the empirical Church, but is present and operative throughout mankind. The Church is not the community of the exclusively saved. Salvation is available for all men, even the unevangelized.

The process of reinterpreting the Church's mission began with the geographical discoveries of the fifteenth century. These made theologians aware of the millions of men cut off from the preaching of the Gospel. St. Thomas could consider the exceptional case of the *puer nutritus in sylvis* and solve the problem by supposing that God by an extraordinary intervention would send an angel or a missionary to reveal the Christian message. While the medievals knew there were peoples outside Christendom, in general they showed little curiosity about them and remained undisturbed by their apparent exclusion from salvation. This detachment was no longer possible when close contact had been established with these peoples. Gradually and with much difficulty, theologians met the problem by applying the concept of implicit faith and charity. To allow that people were saved without grace and without a response to that grace was impossible. But God could work within the conscience of a person and evoke a commitment that transcended a merely natural acknowledgement. How the object of that commitment was conceptualized would greatly vary; obscurity and corruption were to be expected where there was no express revelation. The important factor was that the person should sincerely follow the inner promptings of his conscience, which were in fact the workings of grace, and thus open himself to a reality beyond himself, however vaguely perceived. Only God can read the hearts of men; it is for him to distinguish between a closed self-love and an open and genuine response to his grace. Man's psychology is bafflingly complex, even apart from the mysterious presence of grace. The theological point was that an implicit faith and charity were possible and through them salvation was available to the unevangelized who were sincere.

When the solution is fully applied, it alters the understanding of the Church's relation to the rest of mankind. St. Francis Xavier was urged forward on his missionary journeys by the conviction that unless he brought the Gospel to the pagans they were eternally damned. That simple motive can no longer be invoked. But the matter goes deeper than that. God's purpose for mankind is one. According to that purpose, he intends all men to live in the order of grace. He does not, therefore, postpone his gift of grace to the unevangelized until the end of their lives. He is present to them by grace from the awakening of their moral consciousness. This means that a state of nature with grace absent is in the adult an unrealized hypothesis. In the concrete order, a man is either a sinner rejecting grace or living according to grace as—to use Fr. Karl Rahner's term—an anonymous Christian. Such anonymous or implicit Christianity is not confined to pagans who have never heard of the Gospel. It also describes the state of those in Christian countries whose rejection of Christianity is inculpable. They may know about the Christian message, but for one reason or other its presentation does not confront them with a personal obligation to believe. Their neglect or rejection of it remains compatible with a fundamental openness to grace.

The point should not be exaggerated to exclude the possibility of real unbelief. Men can and presumably do freely close themselves upon themselves and refuse the appeal to open themselves to the transcendent. Some Christians today tend not to admit culpable unbelief as a possible option. Men, however, can choose not to believe. Belief is not always an easy obligation to fulfil, especially for the intellectual. Man's pride resists the call to assent to mysteries outside the mastery of human understanding. Even in human relationships many prefer self-sufficiency to commitment to another. Is it surprising that commitment to God should meet the obstacle of self-regarding love? Men are sinners, and the fact of sin should not be confined to the lower areas of man's experience. Perhaps modern Christians need a greater honesty in admitting the temptation to unbelief within themselves. The reluctance to believe is too easily rationalized as legitimate concern with the updating of Christian teaching. The acknowledgement of the hold unbelief still has upon us and of the failure in our own Christian commitment will lead to a recognition that belief or unbelief is a serious option for our contemporaries. All the same, others cannot judge from appearances. Amid conceptual confusion, there is often a believing commitment. In any case, and this is the important point here, there are no grounds for restricting the response to grace to the minority who belong to the Christian Church.

The order of grace is present universally throughout mankind. It is not confined within the boundaries of the empirical Church. There are secular realities and secular activities, which have their place and autonomy, but when we consider the total lives of men in the concrete, there is no self-contained natural order standing over against the Church. History in the concrete is never a merely secular history unaffected by grace. Even apart from the line of events we call sacred history, the higher integration given by grace is present in history and emerges within the process of man's historical development.

How, then, are we to relate the Church and the world? The difficulty is to tie down the elusive term "world" with its multiple meaning.

The world may be taken in the Johannine sense as the realm of those who have rejected Christ. Anyone who closes himself to grace belongs to that world. It is the kingdom of darkness, ruled over by the Devil. The expression of its power is sin, and through sin it extends its hold upon human life and history, corrupts man's achievements, uses them for evil ends and resists the purifying and integrating effect of grace. Christians believe that the struggle with the forces of evil is real and will continue to the end of time, though Christ has assured the victory. Even those who find the traditional expression of this hard to accept should recognize the fact of moral evil and the way its effects are cumulative, erecting immense obstacles to the spread of moral values and often destroying the finer fruits of man's moral progress.

But the world in this sense cannot be identified with the world of the unchurched. Not only is there through the working of grace a fund of goodness outside the Church, but evil within it. The frontier between the kingdom of darkness and the kingdom of light does not coincide with the boundary of the visible Church. The visible Church does however stand over against the kingdom of darkness, because it is the permanent expression or visibility of the sacred reality of grace and has received Christ's promise that evil will never overcome it. The sins of its members may damage but never totally destroy its holiness as Christ's Church. Unlike that of secular institutions, the opposition between the Church and the world in the Johannine sense is guaranteed within limits.

If the world is understood as the complex of secular realities and activities, then it is distinct from the Church as secular from sacred. There is, however, a close relation between them. The secular world of its nature is open to the higher integration the Church seeks to promote. But when the Church sanctifies the secular world by bringing it under the higher order of grace, it does not sacralize it. There always remains a distinction between the consecrated area of the Church and the area of secular, even if sanctified, realities and activities. That is why the secular is not brought under Church authority, which has the sacred as its sphere and is not concerned with the secular as such but with its integration into the higher order of grace.

To speak of the secular world as such is to name an abstraction. When by the world distinct from the Church is meant the totality of the lives and activities of men outside the Church, then it is not exclusively secular. It is the effect of grace, the product of the universal presence of the sacred among men. Not unambiguously so, because of the corruption due to sin. Nevertheless, Christ is the Lord of history. Despite sin, he is directing human history as a whole to the final Kingdom. His grace is at work everywhere. Sin causes setbacks, false developments and the frequent ruin of the good. Apart from sin, human development of its nature is subject to many vicissitudes. All this prevents a simple view of the course of history. Yet, it remains true that the historical process is a working out of God's plan and a progress towards the Kingdom. God's plan, which is operative through grace, embraces the whole of history, not just the part directly related to the Church.

The world outside the Church includes an achievement of Christ.

The distinction between the Church and the world in the concrete sense described is not a distinction between grace and nature, supernatural and natural, Christian and non-Christian. In so far as the world is good, is it a distinction between the explicitly and implicitly Christian, between a Christianity conscious of itself and an anonymous Christianity, between the epiphany or observable presence of the sacred and the latent presence of the sacred in an externally secular development. There is a double movement of the sacred in history, a two-pronged advance of that higher integration of human living which is given by grace. The first is the explicit revelation of the presence of the mystery, which took place within the historical process by the events constituting sacred history and which has been made permanent in the Church as a consecrated reality. The Church has been set up among men as the visible expression and effectual sign of the sacred. The second movement of the sacred in history is by its latent presence through the working of grace in the consciences of all men. This means that ordinary history is not just secular, but in part sanctified. Underlying its secularity is the hidden presence of the mystery. It, too, is an expression of

the sacred, not of the sacred in itself but in its repercussions upon the secular development of mankind.

This finding demands a more careful look at secular society, understood as an open, pluralist society.
Considered as a secular development, it represents,
I should maintain, an advance in man's social and
political consciousness. Need Christians regard it as
an illusory hope generated by human pride because
the common values on which it is based are not
rooted in a common explicit adherence to the Christian faith? Is it unviable as a social order because
not animated by a common religion? Surely, Christians may regard secular society as in part the effect
of grace on man's development. Its common values,
chiefly the dignity of the human person with all the
freedoms and rights this implies, are not left to the
mercy of man's unaided reason and will. Outside
the Church they are supported by an anonymous
Christianity. Men who are not Christians by name
are helped by God's grace to grasp and pursue those
values. Whatever may be the logical difficulty of
cogently establishing the brotherhood of man without the fatherhood of God, whatever may have been
Christianity's part in introducing the idea to men,
the plain fact is that many who have no clear hold
upon ultimate truth are capable of perceiving that
brotherhood as a value and of promoting it with

energy and integrity, often surpassing Christians in doing so. The same may be said of the other values at the basis of a truly open society. Christians, I suggest, should cease naïvely to expect the immediate establishment of an explicitly Christian society and recognize the slow working out of God's plan within history. They will then no longer be tempted to override the personal freedom of others, but will respect it as God himself does. Secular society is, I maintain, a necessary stage in man's development and—to use a biblical term—a *kairos* for the Christian Church.

Not all parts of time have the same importance. Even from a human standpoint, there are moments of time especially favourable for particular undertakings. In New Testament usage, opportune times or *kairoi* are those created by divine decision. There are points of time that have a special place in the execution of God's plan. Hence the Christian duty of watchfulness. Christians have to scrutinize the signs of the times, so that they may eagerly grasp what opportunity God gives them.

Secular society, I have said, is a *kairos* for the Church. There are several reasons for asserting this. Two have already been mentioned. An open, pluralist society provides the suitable context for the development among Christians of a free, truly personal faith. When prematurely achieved, a Christian society has the effect of stifling this, reducing faith to an imposed, unconsidered social attitude. Next, the secularization of society provokes a Christian awareness of the distinction between secular and sacred, an appreciation of the secular in its relative autonomy and proper value and an enhanced discernment of the sacred in its transcendence. This represents a necessary advance in Christian consciousness, which would have been very difficult to achieve in a stabilized Christian society. How many upheavals have been required for a practical recognition of the distinction between Church and State, between the mission of the Church and politics!

There are, however, two further reasons for regarding the emergence of secular society as an opportune time. In some respects these strike deeper.

Secular society would seem to be the necessary context for the achievement of Christian unity. I do not see the reason for this in Christians being driven together with their backs to the wall to face a hostile world. No; the chief effect of secularization is to check and remove the non-theological causes of Christian divisions. In the past, nationalism, class feeling, economic motives, various social conflicts and tensions have disguised themselves as religious differences. Almost every Christian division has at least a partial explanation on the social, cultural or economic level. Secular conflicts have now no need or temptation to dress themselves up in religious garb; they can openly be what in truth they are. The removal of confusion between sacred and secular allows doctrinal differences to stand out clearly, unaffected by alien distorting influences. Personally I do not think it naïve to say that Christians sincerely seeking unity in Christ should find these differences capable of solution when the issues have been clarified and transitory cultural elements no longer confused with the substance of the Christian faith.

Further, the secularization of the West was needed to allow the Christian Church to become a world Church. This I regard as the key feature in the present situation of Christianity. The present crisis marks the difficult transition from a Western Church to a world Church. As before in its history, the Church is undergoing a death in order to rise again. Christianity has indeed spread over the surface of the globe, but as an extension of the West. It has had no great impact upon other cultures. It has not entered deeply into the lives of the great non-Western peoples. The catholicity of the Church has not yet been actualized in the formation of a Church genuinely belonging to the whole world and not the particular possession of a selected group of peoples. With the unification of mankind, the time has come for the emergence of a world Church. The secularization of the West is a preparation for this.

It is so in two ways. First, the disengagement of the Church from Western society allows Christians to tackle their role in human society on a broader front. While Christians rightly want Christian faith and values to penetrate into a society and thus become embodied in particular societies and cultures, a single, stable embodiment in a particular culture has proved an obstacle to a wider penetration. As long as Christianity was identified with Western society it could not find entry elsewhere. Moreover, it was against all probability that Christians themselves should be able clearly to distinguish between their faith and their culture when both were inextricably intertwined in Christendom. The break-up of Christendom was needed to open the eyes of Christians to a wider horizon. Secular society has freed Christians from a prematurely close involvement that was impeding their worldwide mission.

Second, the secularization of the West has paradoxically had a beneficial effect in the opposite direction. It has increased the influence of the West and is thus, though this is not yet recognized, opening the way for Christianity. The Christian West was unable to break into the enclosed cultures of the East; the secular West is doing so. The present reaction against Western colonialism and political power may here be misleading. Western ideas are spreading throughout the world with increasing rapidity. People may think they can accept Western science and technology and reject the rest. They are mistaken. They do not know what they are handling. They are playing with forces that will break up their cultures in their present form. This need not be seen just negatively as a lamentable destruction. It could well mark an advance into an open, pluralist social order, where ultimate beliefs are freely considered without a cultural exclusiveness. In which case, conditions will have been created suitable for the presentation of the Christian message. That Asia and Africa should make a distinctive cultural contribution is desirable, indeed essential, and is perfectly compatible with an acceptance of Christianity. But they need to learn the distinction between sacred and secular, between religion and culture. It looks as if the secular West is destined to teach them that lesson.

Reflection upon secular society as an opportune time for the Church has not yet answered the question, What is the Church's mission? To that I now return.

There is a double presence of the sacred in history, a two-pronged advance within history towards the final Kingdom. It must now be added that in God's plan the latent presence and its impact upon man's development is dependent upon the manifest presence or explicit revelation of the sacred. This has a twofold meaning. In the first place it is another way of saying that all grace is given through Christ. Christ is the full and definitive revelation of God's self-gift. He is at the centre of sacred history. In him and his work was disclosed the meaning of human history as a whole. He is the Head of mankind and the Lord of history, so that all grace given to men relates them to him. The Church was established as the visible and effectual sign of his permanent presence among men. In the second place, the dependence of the latent upon the manifest presence of the sacred is a statement about the working out of God's plan in history.

The universal, latent presence of grace first ensures that no person is excluded from salvation because the order of grace as a higher integration for human living only slowly emerges within the historical process. It reconciles two apparently conflicting requirements of God's saving plan: first, that salvation should be available to all men; secondly, that the laws of man's historical nature should be respected. The latent presence allows the gift to be offered and the response made, even though only in an implicit form.

Even the latent presence of the sacred will inevitably have a purifying and perfecting influence upon man's development. But that influence is necessarily limited by the lack of a conscious, explicit recognition of the sacred in what distinguishes it from the secular. The sacred cannot have its full intended effect. Hence a further purpose of the latent presence is to widen and reinforce the main impact of the sacred, which comes from its manifest presence. It is through its explicit revelation in sacred history that grace exercises its decisive influence upon man's development. Only through its manifest presence does the sacred have its full effect upon human history. The higher order of grace must emerge in an explicit revelation if it is effectually to integrate human social living and bring mankind as a whole to its ultimate destiny in the Kingdom. But the repercussions of the manifest presence are not confined to those who recognize it. The values it introduces spread among men through countless channels and are taken up with appreciation by many who do not know their origin. The manifest presence acts as a leaven in human society and exerts an influence far beyond the visible community it creates. When its impact upon men thus reaches out far and wide, it is reinforced by the already universal latent presence. Men's appreciation of the values they encounter, unaware though they may be of their origin, is achieved by the working of God's grace within their hearts.

The relation of the manifest and latent presence of God's grace in history determines the role of the Church. The Church is the manifest presence made permanent after the definitive revelation in Christ. It is, therefore, the epiphany of the sacred, the consecrated reality set apart to constitute the visibility of grace. But it is not just a static sign, an explicit revelation intended only for the contemplation of those who recognize it. The Church is at the same time the instrument of the sacred, the means by which it exercises its influence upon man's development. The higher integration given by grace is mediated within history by the Church. The Church is a consecrated people, but a people with a task. It has a mission to the world. Nothing new in that statement. But what is new is the recognition that in carrying out its mission it is acting in conjunction with an already universal but latent presence of grace.

The mission of the Church is twofold.

The first task concerns the sacred in itself. Salvation, I have said, is a transcendent gift. God has solved the human problem by calling man to a higher, supernatural order. The Church has to put the explicit revelation of God's self-communication before men. It has to serve as the instrument of God's self-giving, leading men to an appropriate response that binds them to Christ and to one another in a new communion of love. In brief, its first task is the promotion of faith, hope and charity.

Its second task is the sanctification of the secular. This is concerned with the repercussions of the sacred on every area of human life, bringing all human activity under the higher order of grace, though without destroying its proper nature. Faith, hope and charity are theological virtues, because their purpose is to join man to God as he is in himself. All the same, they have profound social effects. Faith purifies and liberates man's reason and prevents men from aimlessly following after every fashion of thought. Hope counteracts human despair before the tragedy of life. Charity enables men to put aside their grievances, to make a fresh start ever and again, and to recognize that justice without love would soon bring the human enterprise to ruin. Christianity has the potentiality to become a dynamic moral and social force. It is the Church's task to make it so. The Western Church has always been particularly aware of its duty to work in the cause of civilization. There were the incessant labours of those who worked for social order and justice in the Dark Ages that followed the collapse of the Roman Empire in the West. They have always had their imitators in subsequent centuries. Social Christianity, whether represented by the social encyclicals of recent popes or found among such Anglicans as F. D. Maurice, not to mention many men from other Churches, has a long and authentic Christian tradition behind it. Christianity preaches a transcendent gift, but a gift that sanctifies the secular.

The twofold mission of the Church is carried out both directly and indirectly: directly, by the spread of the Christian faith and the extension of the Church; indirectly, in relation with the latent presence of grace, by working with all men of good will in the cause of man's development.

The Church must engage in direct evangelization. It must put the challenge of the Gospel before men, call them to conversion and an explicit faith and build up the visible community of God's People. The direct proclamation of the sacred and the fostering of its manifest presence in a visible Church is an essential part of God's plan. The wider, indirect influence of the Church depends upon it. The entire mission of the Church is founded upon the life of a visible community, consisting of members united by faith and baptism and in communion with one another through the celebration of the Eucharist.

Yet, Christians need now a greater awareness than before that they cannot themselves determine the visible success of direct evangelization. The working out of God's plan in history is a gradual and complex process. There are factors, not implying any bad will in the evangelized, which have and will impede the progress of the Church for centuries. Often a long time must elapse before Christians themselves learn how to present the Gospel effectively in a particular environment. Why, then, the constant surprise at the ups and downs of Church history? What is asked of Christians is faithfulness to their mission. They can leave the determination of visible results to God.

Recognition of the complexity of history has brought into relief the indirect mission of the Church. By direct evangelization the Church both wins explicit acceptance of the sacred and, by the activities of Christian believers, promotes the sanctification of the secular. But there is also a place for

indirect action. Christians work together with those
who are not Christians to solve human problems
and strengthen human values. In doing so, they
respect the secular as secular and encourage its development. They share with others a common humanity and a concern with the secular. But at the
same time they sanctify the secular by bringing to
bear the purifying and integrating power of the
sacred. This is a mission belonging to them precisely as Christians, but their work is supported and
often considerably reinforced by other men, owing
to the latent presence of grace. In working for the
brotherhood of men, social justice, racial equality,
the care and protection of the weak, the humanizing
of cities, personal and social freedom, and so on,
Christians are motivated by the Gospel teaching and
carry out a Christian mission. They make common
cause, however, with many who do not share their
ultimate beliefs. An anxiety to prove the Christian
origin of the values they are working for is out of
place. They should readily admit, that their own
generosity is often surpassed by others'. After all,
they believe in the universal presence of grace.
Their work with others who by their sincerity and
openness are implicitly Christian is sanctifying the
secular. It is also preparing the ground for a wider
explicit acknowledgement of the Christian message,

as this becomes feasible in the historical unfolding of God's plan.

The indirect carrying out of the Church's mission assumes a new importance in secular society. Within such a society particular groups retain and freely express their own convictions. They are not expected to restrict themselves to a lowest common denominator of beliefs and values. They may initiate ideas and seek to win acceptance for them. What they are required to do is to work by reasonable discussion and persuasion, not by attempts to override the convictions of others. Christians, then, are not only free to preach the Gospel; they have a good opportunity of leading others to accept many values that can be perceived as good without necessarily becoming Christians. To try to do this tests their own appreciation of those values, and they will also find that they have much to learn about them from others.

A secular society cannot exist without tensions. There are bound to be clashes of conviction. To overcome these amicably and with as much tolerance as public order permits is admittedly difficult. The contention, however, is not that secular society is an easy achievement, but that it is a social order worth trying to attain. While accepting it, Christians must expect frequently to be a sign of contradiction. If they are true to their mission, they will constantly find themselves in opposition to what is fashionable and commonly accepted. Christ gave them no assurance that their witness would be popular; indeed, he warned them to expect contempt and persecution. Perhaps it is worth recalling, however, that to be a sign of contradiction does not mean to adopt an attitude of aggressive hostility towards others, but patiently to bear mockery and worse for courageously sticking to one's convictions. Intolerance has always been a remarkable inference to draw from the example of Christ.

The traditional three functions of the Church may now be interpreted in relation to its direct and indirect mission. First, teaching: the Church directly proclaims and teaches the Christian message; indirectly it spreads it by joining with non-Christians in bearing witness to values they also can and do perceive. Ministry: the Church directly carries out its ministry by building up the Christian community and exercising all the functions this demands; indirectly its ministry includes a general service of mankind, which it shares with all who are working for human welfare. Communion or fellowship: the Church directly seeks to maintain and foster a visible communion among Christians as the sacrament or effectual sign of Christ's salvation and the manifest presence of the sacred; its further or indirect mission is to work with all men of good will for peace and love among men, for the practical recognition by everyone of the unity of mankind.

The long analysis I have given of the mission of the Church leads me to risk a few remarks about "religionless Christianity." As popularly understood, whatever Bonhoeffer himself may have intended, it seems to me to express two true insights, but in a onesided and falsely exclusive way.

The first insight is that the empirical or institutional Church with its array of functions and organized worship is a means not an end. The end is the progress of the order of grace among men through faith, hope and charity, until the higher integration intended by God for mankind is finally achieved in the Kingdom. When God gives the final fulfilment, the institutional Church will cease. Hence it should never be made an end in itself. In a difficult situation the Church is sometimes tempted to compromise its mission in order to save its institutional existence. To do so is to betray Christ. Its permanence as a visible community has in fact been guaranteed. All the more reason why it should not fear to risk its own survival when the end for which it exists demands this. "Religionless Christianity" expresses an impatience with a Christian religion turned in upon itself and concerned only with the preservation and working of its own inner system. But it exaggerates in forgetting the indispensable role of the Church as the manifest presence of the sacred in history. The foundation for all Christian mission is the visible community with its life.

The second true insight the phrase contains is that what I have called the indirect mission of the Church is of exceptional importance at the present time. The commitment of Christians to working with others in secular society for human values is a key part of their mission today. They must go out of an insulated Christian environment and meet God's grace as it is operative among their fellow citizens. They should cease to bewail modern society and try to appreciate the genuine achievements of modern secular man, while discerning his still persistent needs and longings. "Religionless Christianity" expresses an impatience with a Christianity that rejects the world. But it is an exaggerated reaction that forgets that grace is not nature, that God offers men a transcendent gift and that his gift is made manifest to men in the historical Church. The mission of the Church can never be reduced to a supporting of the secular.

History, I have already remarked, is an open-ended process. It does not follow a necessary path. In particular, it allows for a variety of free, human choices. This is true of the impact of Christianity and the gradual emergence within history of the higher order of grace. There is room for man's free preferences. Christian principles can be made concrete and effective in multiple ways. The gift of grace does not stifle man's creative intelligence. So, there is no such thing in the course of history as *the* Christian order. We can never point to *the* Christian society, *the* Christian culture, *the* Christian political system, and so on. The Christian pattern can always be embodied differently. This is certainly true of any partial Christian achievements history may bring. It is, however, also true of the final order, which, though God's gift, will bear the mark of man's creative intelligence and free choice. What it will be like we cannot say. But we do know that it will be sacred because centred on the completion of God's self-communication through Christ and secular because it will be the fulfilment, not the destruction, of man's nature.

INDEX

agnosticism, 16
agriculture, 27f.
authority, 89f.
 sacred and secular, 35f.

Bonhoeffer, Dietrich, 122

Chenu, M. D., 73
Christ, 24, 57, 106
 at the centre of sacred history, 55
 at the head of mankind, 56
 resurrection, 69
 all grace is given through him, 113
Christendom
 Western, 35f.
Christian Church, 74–76
 mission, 9–10, 18–19, 35, 83–87, 99–124
 history, 9–10, 35, 78–82
 and State, distinguishing between, 26, 35, 109
 renewal, 38

structure, 89–99
 the visible expression of the sacred, 106
 consecrated reality, 115
 instrument of the sacred, 116
 institutional; a means not an end, 122
Christianity, 26–27, 73–85, 124
 authentic, 10
 presentation of, 17
 distinguishes radically between sacred and secular, 24
 breaks down enclosed sacral cultures, 24
 a newer and higher integration of the life of men, 69–70, 76
 religionless, 123–124
 Christianity in World History (van Leeuwen), 25
Christians
 attitudes to secularization, 16–17